CITIES OF THE WORLD

MONTREAL

BY STILLMAN D. ROGERS

CHILDREN'S PRESS®
A Division of Grolier Publishing
New York London Hong Kong Sydney
Danbury, Connecticut

CONSULTANTS

Gilles Bengle
Director, Media Relations
Tourisme Montréal

Linda Cornwell
Coordinator of School Quality and Professional Improvement
Indiana State Teachers Association

Project Editor: Downing Publishing Services
Design Director: Karen Kohn & Associates, Ltd.
Photo Researcher: Jan Izzo
Pronunciations: Courtesy of Tony Breed, M.A., Linguistics, University of Chicago

---

NOTES ON FRENCH PRONUNCIATION

Zh is like *s* in pleasure; *gh* is always like *g* in get. Some vowels are very much like vowels in English; *igh* is as in high; *ee* is as in bee, *ay* is as in day, *eh* or *e* is as *e* in bet, *ah* or *a* is as *a* in father, *aw* is as in draw, *oh* is as *o* in open, and *oo* is always as in boot. The sound *uh* is like *oo* in book, but much shorter and quicker. Some sounds in French do not occur in English: Notice how you hold your lips to say *oo*, and then notice where you put your tongue to say *ee*; now, to pronounce *ew*, hold your lips to say *oo* but move your tongue forward to say *ee*. To say *ooh* is similar; say *ooh* as in book, but move your tongue forward to say *ay*.

Visit Children's Press on the Internet at: http://publishing.grolier.com

Library of Congress Cataloging-in-Publication Data
Rogers, Stillman D.
    Montreal / by Stillman D. Rogers.
        p. cm. — (Cities of the world)
    Includes bibliographical references and index.
    Summary: Describes the history, culture, daily life, food, people, sports, and points of interest in this large French-speaking city in southern Quebec, Canada.
    ISBN 0-516-21637-6 (lib. bdg.)   0-516-27038-9 (pbk.)
    1. Montreal (Québec)—Juvenile literature.   [1. Montreal (Québec)] I. Title.
II. Series: Cities of the world (New York, N.Y.)
    F1054.5.M84R64   2000   99-33908
    971.4'2804—dc21   CIP
    ROG

GROLIER
PUBLISHING

TABLE OF CONTENTS

Montreal's streets slope downhill to the river, and on weekends they seem to spill Montrealers onto the two green islands below. Île Ste-Hélène and Île Notre-Dame, in the middle of the St. Lawrence River, are covered in grass and trees, with a beach for swimming, paths for bicycling and in-line skating, and acres of gardens to walk in. These islands seem miles away from the cars and buildings and busy streets of Montreal.

Montreal (MAWN-TRAY-AHL)
Île Ste-Hélène (EEL SAHNT-AY-LEN)
Île Notre-Dame (EEL NOH-TRUH-DAHM)

The twin islands of Ste-Hélène and Notre-Dame, where Montrealers now play, have not always been there. When French explorers first sailed up the St. Lawrence River and were stopped by the fast-flowing white waters of Lachine Rapids, they saw only one island. The second of these explorers, Samuel de Champlain, named it Île Ste-Hélène in honor of his wife, Hélène.

Ste-Hélène sat there alone until 1966, when Montreal was busy preparing for all the visitors coming to the big international show, Expo 67. As workers dug tunnels for the new subway system, they carried 28 million tons of rock and dirt from under downtown streets and dumped it in the river to create Île Notre-Dame. Some of the rock was used to make Île Ste-Hélène even bigger.

Buckminster Fuller's geodesic dome on Île Ste-Hélène, built for Expo 67, is now an environmental exhibition center devoted to the St. Lawrence River and Great Lakes ecosystem.

Lachine (LAH-SHEEN)
Samuel de Champlain
(SAH-MEW-EL DUH SHAHM-PLAN)
Rivière des Prairies
(REEVE-YARE DAY PREH-REE)

The Old Fort on Île Ste-Hélène (left) houses a military and maritime museum that puts on military parades with participants dressed in eighteenth-century costumes (below).

Expo 67 brought together more than 60 nations, each with a pavilion showing the world its culture, foods, history, and latest achievements. More than 50 million visitors came to Montreal during the summer of 1967, from countries all around the world.

The islands of Ste-Hélène and Notre-Dame are a reminder that the city itself is on an island. Shaped like a boomerang, this island is 32 miles (51 kilometers) long and more than 10 miles (16 km) wide at its center. It is surrounded by the St. Lawrence, the Rivière des Prairies, and two lakes. And like the islands at its feet, Montreal is constantly changing.

FACES

People have been mixing in Montreal almost since its beginning. While these different cultures blend into a rich ethnic stew, they do not lose their identity or separate character. This makes Montreal a colorful and interesting city, and a visit there is almost like going on a mini-tour of the whole world.

Above: A magnet with the symbols of Montreal, including a fleur-de-lis, a lily, and a shamrock

OLD MONTREAL

The first foreigners to settle here were the French, and Old Montreal, where their city began, still has a very French flavor. Its narrow cobbled streets rise from the waterfront opposite Île Ste-Hélène to the crest of a hill. Here the Hôtel de Ville, or city hall, stands looking grandly down on busy Place Jacques-Cartier.

This square, filled with sidewalk cafés, street entertainers, and vendors under bright umbrellas, is the heart of Old Montreal. Around it are streets lined by some of Montreal's oldest buildings, which now house shops, art galleries, and restaurants.

Forty years ago, these old stone buildings were crumbling and empty. No one wanted to live in them, and some had already been torn down to build tall, modern office buildings. But Montrealers didn't want to lose these reminders of their past, and in 1962 they formed the Viger Commission to preserve and restore the old city.

Now, no one can tear down a building here, and even inside changes must preserve its history. Today, it is one of the most fashionable neighborhoods for apartments.

Place Jacques-Cartier, a square filled with sidewalk cafés, street entertainers, and vendors is the heart of Old Montreal.

Hôtel de Ville (OH-TELL DUH VEE)
Place Jacques-Cartier (PLAHSS ZHAHCK CART-YAY)

Close to Old Montreal, Chinatown is entered through giant gates. Chinese people came to work on the Canadian Pacific Railway in the 1800s. The community today is also home to Koreans, Cambodians, Vietnamese, Thais, and others from Asia. On Saturdays and Sundays, crowds fill the busy street markets. While parents shop, children play in Sun Yat Sen Park, near the big gate on Rue de La Gauchetière.

While Clark and de La Gauchetière streets may look like a scene from Hong Kong, just a few blocks away, Rue St-Denis could be in Paris. Sidewalk café tables, bistros, chic shops, and round kiosks covered with posters mark Montreal's center of French arts, culture, and nightlife.

Montreal's Chinatown is entered through giant gates.

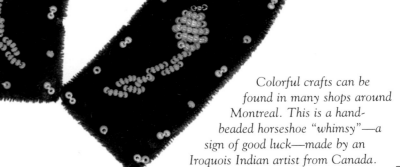

Colorful crafts can be found in many shops around Montreal. This is a hand-beaded horseshoe "whimsy"—a sign of good luck—made by an Iroquois Indian artist from Canada.

Rue de La Gauchetière (REW DEH LAH GOH-SHETT-YARE)
Rue St-Denis (REW SAHN DEH-NEE)

NEW MONTREAL

Not all the city's architecture is old. Some of the best modern architecture in the world is in Montreal's downtown, northwest of Old Montreal. Near its center, the Château Champlain Hotel is called "the cheese grater" because of its tall shape and unusual rounded windows.

All around downtown are other fascinating shapes and textures of new architectural styles. Some streets are like canyons between the sleek glass walls of modern buildings filled with offices, stores, and banks. Here, too, are museums, McGill University, and Place des Arts, where concert halls and theaters surround a plaza with a pool and fountains.

Winters in Montreal last three cold, snowy months. So when the city built the Metro subway system, they thought it would be nice if people could get from subway stops to other places without having to go outdoors.

A Montreal resident

A view of downtown Montreal

The Montreal skyline at night

The maple leaf (below) is one of the symbols of Canada.

Place des Arts (PLAHSS DAY ZAR)

Getting Around

Montreal is an easy city to get around in because it is laid out in a grid, like a checkerboard. The subway system, called the Metro, is neat and clean and moves people quickly to all corners of the city. Aboveground, buses take them to places in between subway stops. The Metro even goes under the river to Île Ste-Hélène and Île Notre-Dame.

Their plans have since grown into 22 miles (34 km) of walkways leading underground to the major hotels, offices, and museums. Three huge shopping malls burrow five stories under downtown, connected to big department stores such as The Bay.

One of the biggest of these malls is on Rue Ste-Catherine, right under the stone Christ Church Cathedral. A big picture in the mall shows how the huge church was lifted and the mall and underground city were built below it.

Escalators take people from floor to floor inside gigantic atriums that let in light from the sky. Some of the atriums have fountains and "sidewalk" cafés. In the summer, the underground city is cool and comfortable, and in winter, people can walk around in shirtsleeves.

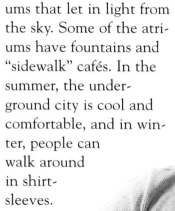

One of the biggest underground malls is directly below the stone Christ Church Cathedral, shown above.

A Montreal resident

Rue Ste-Catherine (REW SAHNT CAH-TREEN)
Molson Centre (MOLE-SAWN SAWN-TRUH)

Montrealers like to meet in the food courts here, and go shopping together. The underground even links up with apartment buildings and the Molson Centre, new home of the Montreal Canadiens, the city's famous hockey team.

Place Montreal Trust, an above-ground, indoor shopping complex, is an alternative to the shopping malls in the underground city.

A CITY ON THE HILL

Downtown Montreal climbs the slopes of Mont-Royal (Mount Royal), the mountain that gave the city its name. Streets also climb to flat highlands called the Plateau. Many groups of immigrants have settled in this part of the city, and today more people live in a smaller area there than any place else in Canada.

You might expect this heavy concentration of people to live in huge, many-storied apartment buildings or in crowded slums. But the Plateau has neither tall buildings nor slums. Instead, people live in clean, pleasant neighborhoods of two- and three-story houses.

An elegant neighborhood on the hillside of Mount Royal

Mont-Royal
(MAWN RWAH-YAHL)
Jean-Talon
(ZHAHN TAH-LAWN)

North of the Plateau is a section called Little Italy because of the Italian families who began immigrating there in the mid-1800s. Small stores sell Italian groceries; restaurants and cafés serve Italian foods; and even the churches and parks look like those in Italy. The busy Jean-Talon Market is in the heart of Little Italy.

In the late 1800s, immigrants from Russia, Poland, Germany, and other Baltic countries came, hoping to work as log cutters in the forests north of Montreal.

Among them were many Jews, and the community they formed as newcomers is still home to Jewish families. During the fall harvest holidays of Sukkot, small, temporary, wooden huts can be seen on Jewish homes, usually above the front porch.

During the fall harvest festival of Sukkot, small wooden huts can be seen on Jewish homes in Montreal.

A Montreal mother and her children

In the 1960s, many Portuguese settled into the Plateau near Rachel, Roy, and Drolet streets. In their colorful neighborhoods of brightly painted houses, Portuguese restaurants and shops sell daily newspapers from Portugal.

Visitors to Montreal's residential neighborhoods always comment on the rows and rows of outdoor stairways. In order to save space inside crowded homes, people built the stairways to upper floors on the outside of the house.

Rachel (RAH-SHELL)
Roy (RWAH)
Drolet (DROH-LAY)

Brightly painted houses in the Portuguese section of the Plateau

Later homes continued this style, with graceful staircases curving to reach upper-floor apartments. These buildings are found all over Montreal, but especially on the Plateau.

In the late 1800s, so many wealthy people built mansions along Sherbrooke and neighboring streets west of the Plateau that it was called the Golden Square Mile. Many of the ornate old mansions remain today. Some are still residences, others now house hotels and smart shops.

To save indoor space, graceful curving staircases that reach to upper-floor apartments are built outside many Montreal houses.

A young Montrealer in sunglasses and a warm jacket

Long before Europeans came to this part of the New World, the site of Montreal was already a city. The Huron tribe of Native Americans (called "First Peoples" by Canadians) lived in a palisaded settlement called Hochelaga. Between the mountain and the river, they built dwellings around a central plaza.

Hochelaga (OASH-LAH-GAH)

THE FRENCH HERITAGE BEGINS

Like many other navigators and explorers of the 1500s, Jacques Cartier was looking for a new route to China when he sailed into the St. Lawrence River on his 1534–35 voyage from France. After stopping at a tiny camp where Quebec City would soon stand, he sailed 165 miles (266 km) up the river to Hochelaga.

Cartier climbed the mountain behind the village, naming it Mont-Real (Mount Royal). From there, he could see the wide silver thread of river flowing into the distant west. But powerful rapids kept him from sailing farther, and he left on the same day. The part

Jacques Cartier (above) had his first interview with the First Peoples at Hochelaga (now Montreal) in 1535 (left).

Jacques Cartier (ZHAHCK CART-YAY)
Quebec (KWIH-BECK)

Trappers watching for otters for the fur trade

of the St. Lawrence that stopped him is now called Lachine (China) Rapids, a reference to Cartier's goal.

Hochelaga wasn't visited by Europeans again until 1603, when Samuel de Champlain was also stopped by the rapids. When Champlain returned to Canada in 1608, he founded the city of Quebec and began to trade with the First Peoples for furs.

Fur trade and missionary work with Indians led Paul de Chomedey, Sieur de Maisonneuve, and a band of 41 people to settle at the foot of Mount Royal in 1642. The new town, named Ville-Marie de Montreal, became the center of the fur trade and of all commerce with the west. Sieur de Maisonneuve's goal was to teach the Catholic faith to the Indians.

Champlain (SHAHM-PLAN)
Paul de Chomedey, Sieur de Maisonneuve
(POLE DUH SHOAM-DAY, SYOOHR DUH MAY- ZONE OOHV)
Ville-Marie de Montreal
(VEE MAH-REE DUH MAWN-TRAY-AHL)
Musée Pointe-a-Calliere
(MEW-ZAY PWANT-AH-CAH-YARE)

Seeing Early Montreal

Montrealers can step back in time and walk on the same streets the First Peoples and early settlers walked, seeing Ville-Marie as archaeologists uncover it. At Musée Pointe-a-Calliere, visitors can go underground where original street pavements and foundations, brick sewer pipes, and even a cemetery have lain buried for hundreds of years.

POINTE-À-CALLIÈRE

Musée d'archéologie et d'histoire de Montréal

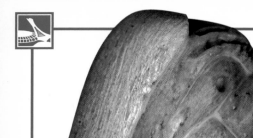

When Samuel de Champlain began the colony of New France, the major Native American groups along the river were the Algonquin, the Huron, and their enemy, the Iroquois. Champlain made a treaty with the Algonquin and Huron to help defend them from Iroquois attacks. Until a treaty in 1701, fierce fighting continued with the Iroquois. The small outpost of Ville-Marie withdrew behind its palisades.

Among the pioneers who came with Paul de Chomedey, Jeanne Mance and Marguerite de Bourgeoys began a tradition of civic responsibility that has lasted until today. They worked to help both settlers and First Peoples. In 1645, Jeanne Mance founded the first hospital in Canada to care for the sick and those injured during wars with the Iroquois.

An Iroquois statue

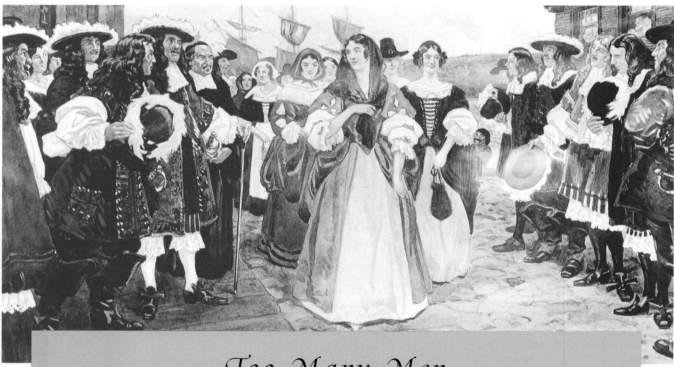

Too Many Men

By 1655, there were 719 single men in the colony but only 65 single women. The French king, Louis XIV, solved the problem by giving a dowry to orphan girls who would go to the colony to marry. More than 700 of these *"Filles du Roi"* (Daughters of the King) came to Marguerite de Bourgeoys' home, the Maison St-Gabriel.

This surprise attack by Champlain on an Iroquois camp was part of the ongoing fighting with the Iroquois.

Marguerite de Bourgeoys saw the need for education and founded the teaching order of Sisters of the Congregation of Notre Dame. In 1658, she opened the first school for women in New France in a converted stable. Much of what is known of the daily life and hardships of the first settlers was learned from her diaries. Stained-glass portraits in Notre-Dame Basilica pay tribute to Jeanne Mance and Marguerite de Bourgeoys.

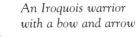

An Iroquois warrior with a bow and arrow

Jeanne Mance
(ZHAHNN MAHNSS)
Marguerite de Bourgeoys
(MAR-GUH-REET DUH BOORZH-WA)
Filles du Roi
(FEE DEW RWAH)
Maison St-Gabriel
(MAY-ZAWN SAHN-GAH-BREE-ELL)

25

ENGLAND RULES MONTREAL

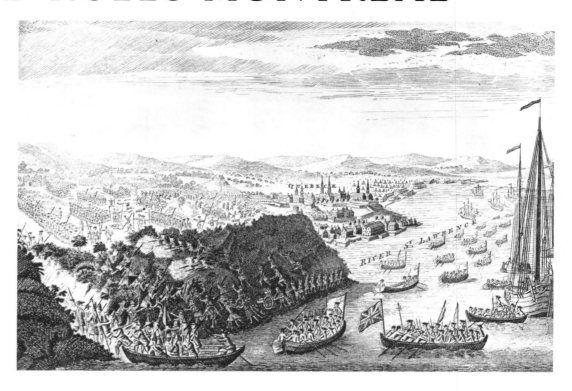

Competition between France and England for control of Europe spilled over into North America in the 1700s. The French along the St. Lawrence River and the British, who controlled the thirteen colonies to the south, fought for control of North America while their parent countries fought at home. French and Indian attacks on British outposts in New England led to British attacks on French Canada.

Both wanted to control the St. Lawrence River. In 1758, when the British seized the great French fort of Louisbourg in Cape Breton, they marched on Quebec City, capturing it in 1759. France's empire in North America ended in 1760 when the British captured Montreal.

With British victory, the French leaders returned to France. They left ordinary settlers, called *habitants*, to deal with life under their old enemy, England. Fortunately for them (and for the British), the first British royal governor, General James Murray, respected the hardy settlers and kept much of the French system of laws and government that they were used to. Changes were few for the habitants, but British rule brought them only a short peace.

By the 1770s, rebellion in the thirteen British colonies south of Canada was in full swing. Leaders of the new United States began to look north, thinking that the French would want to throw off their British rulers and join the revolt.

British commander James Wolfe, with a fleet of ships and 4,000 men, captured Quebec City from the French in 1759.

General James
Wolfe was killed
during the battle for
Quebec City.

Louisbourg
(LOO-EE-BOORG)
Cape Breton
(CAPE BRETT-UN)
habitants
(AH-BEE-TAHN)

On November 13, 1775, only eight months after the first shots of the American Revolution were fired, Americans under General Richard Montgomery captured Montreal. But French citizens did not rally to help the American invaders. After a bitter winter, American troops withdrew from the city in the spring of 1776.

Montreal became the headquarters for British attempts to split the thirteen American colonies in half. The area between the St. Lawrence and Lake Champlain became a battleground, but the British failed to divide the colonies. By 1812, the Americans and the British were at war again. There were battles near Montreal, and the Americans talked of invading Canada.

During the American Civil War, England and its Canadian colony supported the Confederate states and tensions once again rose along the border. It was fear of American threats that led the British to create a single confederation called Canada from the colonies of Ontario, Quebec, Nova Scotia, and New Brunswick in 1867.

The St. Lawrence River continued to influ-

The Civil War in Vermont

In 1864, during the American Civil War, 22 Confederate soldiers sneaked into tiny St. Albans, Vermont, from the area south of Montreal. On October 19, they robbed local banks of more than $200,000, which was a huge sum for the time, and killed one man before escaping back into Canada. This was the northernmost land raid of the war.

In 1760, when the British seized control of Montreal, France's empire in North America ended.

ence Montreal and became the source of its wealth. In the 1820s, a canal bypassed the Lachine Rapids and by 1885 the Canadian Pacific Railway was completed between Montreal and the Pacific Ocean. Settlers in the western prairies began growing wheat and other grains, which they shipped by boat and train to Montreal. Huge grain elevators rose along the shore, and Montreal thrived as a commercial center.

Passengers aboard a sleeping car on the Canadian Pacific Railway

An early Canadian locomotive

ONE NATION, TWO PEOPLE

When the British captured French Canada in 1758–1760 they took control of a large and well-established Roman Catholic colony. To keep the French habitants happy, the British Parliament in 1774 established French civil law and guaranteed the right of French citizens to practice the Roman Catholic faith.

Although the habitants had refused to join the Americans in the Revolution, they also took little interest in helping the British against the Americans. Even many years later when Britain fought Germany in World War I, few French Canadians volunteered to protect the British Empire.

This early scene on the St. Lawrence River shows Montreal in the distance.

This split between the two great cultures of Quebec province, and between French Quebec and the rest of Canada, remains to this day. Separatist movements have gained and lost strength over the years. Elections to decide if Quebec should leave Canada and create a new country lost closely enough in the 1980s and 1990s to keep the hopes of separatist Québécois alive.

Even though French-speaking Quebec has sent many of its outstanding leaders to head the Canadian government as premier, and even though the French dominate all the offices of their province, some francophones in Montreal still fear that the ancient British enemy will crush the French heritage they love.

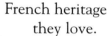

Above: Quebec premier Lucien Bouchard, first elected in 1996, is head of the separatist Parti Québécois and wants the separation of Quebec from Canada.

Right: Daniel Johnson, Quebec premier from 1994 to 1996, represented the Liberal Party and believes Quebec should remain a part of Canada.

Québécois (KAY-BECK-WAH)

While Montreal is proud of its rich French heritage, everyone also enjoys the city's other cultures. Montrealers love a good time, especially when it includes food and music, so whenever there's a neighborhood festival, the streets are crowded with people.

FOOD AND CELEBRATIONS

Montrealers love to buy fresh food grown on the farms of neighboring Laval to the north and on the south shore in their own province of Quebec. In the city's markets, where farmers gather to sell their fruits and vegetables, signs announce to shoppers that the tomatoes or peppers are *"Produito du Québec"* (Produce from Quebec).

The two largest city markets are Atwater, near the Lachine Canal, and Jean-Talon, in the heart of Little Italy. Shops inside the markets and outdoor stalls sell farm produce, meat, fresh fish, and other foods. One shop in Atwater sells nothing but cheese, another's specialty is oils and vinegars. Cafés in the markets serve morning breakfasts of pastry or a fresh crusty baguette with *cretons*, a delicious spread made of spiced pork.

Smoked meat is another Montreal specialty, known throughout Canada. Similar to pastrami, it is a legacy of Jewish immigrants from Romania, and in Montreal it is eaten with french fries and dill pickles.

Montrealers love festivals and celebrations. Starting in spring and continuing throughout the summer, they host the Formula I Grand Prix; the International Fireworks Competition; the International Jazz Festival; a festival of laughter (*Festival Juste Pour Rire*) with comedy shows; a festival of French music called the *Franco Folies*; and the *Festival International des Films du Monde* (Films of the World festival).

Laval (LAH-VAHL)
café (CAH-FAY)
baguette (BAH-GET)
cretons (CREH-TAWN)

Above: A small child sitting on pumpkins at Atwater Market

Left: An Atwater Market vendor holding a ham

Above: A fruit and vegetable stall at the Jean-Talon Market in the heart of Little Italy

Left: The Festival Juste Pour Rire (Festival of Laughter)

Festival Juste Pour Rire
(FESS-TEE-VAHL ZHEWST POOR REER)
Franco Folies (FRAHN-KOH FOH-LEE)
Festival International des Films du Monde
(FESS-TEE-VAHL AN-TARE-NAHSS-YOH-NAHL DAY FEELM DEW
MOAND)

The two biggest festivals are held in winter and summer. In February, the great big fuzzy polar bear, *Boule de Neige,* comes out of hibernation to rule over Montreal's *Fête des Neiges* in Parc Jean-Drapeau, on the island of Ste-Hélène. Families come to the island from all around Montreal to celebrate winter.

A special sledding and tubing hill is built, and people can ride in sleighs pulled by horses or

Left: The big fuzzy polar bear Boule de Neige *entertaining children at the* Fête des Neiges

dogsleds pulled by huskies. The centerpiece of the festival are the ice sculptures. Everyone climbs onto a huge ice fortress and visits the animals inside a Noah's Ark built of ice. People who haven't tried cross-country skiing or walked on snowshoes can learn at the *Fête des Neiges*, and even rent equipment. Skating rinks are everywhere.

At the Old Fort, men in costumes of the early French settlers demonstrate curling. This sport is played on ice, using heavy curling stones.

In June and July, the night sky erupts with light and color during the *Competition Internationale d'Art Pyrotechnique*, the International Fireworks Competition. Fireworks makers from all over the world come to Île Ste-Hélène to show off their best and most exciting displays. Many people view the fireworks from special viewing stands in La Ronde Amusement Park; others watch from the Jacques Cartier Bridge, which is closed to traffic for the show.

Not all celebrations are city-wide festivals like these. Family events such as christenings and weddings are also reason for everyone to celebrate. On weekends, the park between the Hôtel de Ville and the court building may be filled with wedding parties.

Fireworks light up the sky during the International Fireworks Competition in June and July.

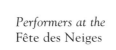

Performers at the Fête des Neiges

Boule de Neige (BOOL DUH NEZH)
Fête des Neiges (FETT DAY NEZH)
International d'Art Pyrotechnique
(AN-TARE-NAHSS-YOH-NAHL DAR PEE-ROE-TECK-NEEK)
La Ronde (LAH-RAWND)

A CITY OF PARKS

When Montrealers are not enjoying one of the neighborhood festivals, they often use the city's dozens of parks and outdoor spaces. The St. Lawrence River gives Montreal a wide "front yard." Along the river in Old Montreal is a wide promenade, a green park with sidewalks and benches where people sit to watch the boats on the river. Many workers in nearby shops and offices eat their lunch by the river.

The waterfront is always a good place to find activity. Boats take people on exciting rides over the Lachine Rapids—something Cartier and Champlain couldn't do—and other boats cruise up and down the river. Nearby is the dock where ferry boats leave to cross the river or go to Île Ste-Hélène. Many people take the ferry back and forth just for the ride. In Parc Bassin

Rafting on the Lachine Rapids

Young Montrealers enjoying a sunny summer day at the waterfront

Bonsecours, on the river near the Bonsecours Market, children and adults often fly kites. In the winter, they skate near boats frozen into the river's ice.

From Montreal's combined French and British heritage comes the city's love of flowers. In spring, summer, and fall, parks and gardens all over the city are covered with bright blossoms. Each year, the city gives plants to homeowners and holds contests to honor the best gardens.

In spring, summer, and fall, parks and gardens all over Montreal are covered with flowers.

Parc Bassin Bonsecours (PARK BAH-SAN BAWN-SEH-COOR)

A LOVE OF SPORTS

The game of ice hockey began in Nova Scotia and Montreal in the 1870s. It is the favorite sport of Montrealers—and of most Canadians. Nearly every boy and many girls learn to play, and to play well, almost from the time they begin to walk. When there is no ice for skating, neighborhood teams play hockey on the pavements.

Although Montreal has designed its downtown so people don't have to go outside in the cold, the rest of the city encourages everyone to enjoy winter. When snow and ice cover the ground, the walking and running paths in Parc Maisonneuve, near the Olympic Stadium, become cross-country ski trails. One huge oval track there turns into a public skating trail. People without skates and skis can

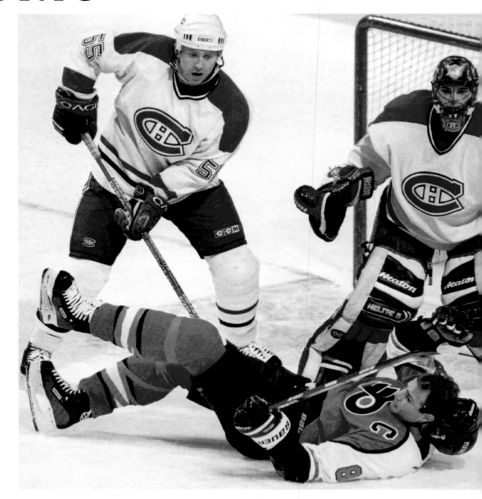

Action at a hockey game between the Canadiens and the Philadelphia Flyers

A hockey stick

The National League Montreal Expos are the city's baseball team.

Parc Maisonneuve
(PARK MAY-ZONE-OOHV)
Parc Lafontaine
(PARK LAH-FAWN-TEN)
Canadiens (CAH-NAHD-YEN)
Les Habitants (LAY-ZAH-BEE-TAHN)
Alouettes (AH-LOO-ETT)

rent them at a large warm-up building in the park.

Everywhere you look in winter, you will see Montrealers on skates. There is skating in Mont-Royal Park, on the mountain, and in a great long winding pond in Parc Lafontaine on the Plateau. These are just a few of the dozens of public rinks and ponds kept clear of snow for skaters. Montreal also designates public sledding hills for the winter.

It is no wonder that hockey is the king of sports in this city and that the Montreal Canadiens are the king of kings. Montrealers call their team in blue and red sweaters the "Habs" (short for "Les Habitants"), even though its official name is the Canadiens. The Habs used to play in the Forum. They now play downtown in the bigger and more modern Molson Centre.

If hockey is king then baseball is queen in sports-loving Montreal. The city is proud of the record of its favorite, the Montreal Expos, who are in the National League. They play in the Olympic Stadium.

The Montréal Alouettes are the home football team. But football at McGill Stadium is not reserved just for the team, and it is common to see both men and women students playing a pick-up game between the goalposts in the middle of their downtown campus.

A hockey puck

THE ARTS

This city of two languages enjoys music and art, which they can share in any language. A complex downtown on Rue Ste-Catherine provides a home for performing arts. Called the Place des Arts, the buildings have concert halls and stages for the Orchestre Symphonique de Montréal, the Grand Ballet of Canada, and L'Opéra de Montréal, world-class companies that perform there regularly.

All over the city, other talented performers play in churches and halls, and sing or act in clubs. The center for French-language arts is in the Latin Quarter along Rue St-Denis.

The Illuminated Crowd, *by English sculptor Raymond Mason, can be seen at the National Bank of Paris.*

Orchestre Symphonique de Montréal (OAR-KESS-TRUH SIM-FOE-NEEK DUH MAWN-TRAY-AHL)
L'Opéra de Montréal (LOH-PARE-AH DUH MAWN-TRAY-AHL)
Musée d'Art Contemporain de Montréal (MEW-ZAY DAR CONE-TEM-POH-RAN DUH MAWN-TRAY-AHL)
Musée des Beaux Arts (MEW-ZAY DAY BOH ZAR)
Rue University (REWYOO-NIH-VER-SIT-EE)
Floralies (FLOH-RAH-LEE)
Yves Trudeau (EVE TREW-DOE)

The Place des Arts

Also in the Place des Arts is the Musée d'Art Contemporain de Montréal, specializing in art created since 1940 from Quebec and from around the world. It is the only Canadian museum dedicated to contemporary art. On Rue Sherbrooke, older works—especially those of Canadian artists—are shown at the Musée des Beaux Arts. This museum has a number of paintings by the famed Canadian "Group of Seven" and by Canadian painter James Wilson Morrice.

Most cities have statues to honor famous people or events, but Montreal carries its public sculpture much further. Some streets, like Avenue McGill College, are like outdoor art galleries. The most controversial public sculpture is of a large group of people, made of white polymer. They all seem to be looking at some terrible thing across the street. Opposite, life-sized bronze figures of a boy and girl sit on a park bench. Nearby, an elk stands listening to the passing traffic.

A terrace at the Canadian Center for Architecture is filled with sculpture made of bits of buildings. Arches, chimneys, columns, and even windows and doorways rise along the paths above a rose garden.

Other gardens are the setting for sculpture, too. On Île Notre-Dame in the Floralies Gardens are works of modern artists including

Alexander Calder, Sebastian, and Yves Trudeau. Even the statues representing historic people are creative in Montreal, such as the one of the founder of McGill University, which stands on the campus. His coat blows behind him as though caught in Montreal's winter wind.

Bronze figures of a boy and girl on a park bench can be seen on Avenue McGill College.

Visitors usually begin a tour where the city itself began, exploring the quaint narrow streets along the river in Old Montreal, with their old-world atmosphere.

But Montreal's sights are not just for the 10 million tourists who come each year. Local families enjoy its museums, gardens, and historic places, and even take rides in the colorful *caleches*, or horse-drawn carriages.

caleche (CAH-LESH)

OLD MONTREAL AND DOWNTOWN

The towers of the Chapel of Notre-Dame-de-Bonsecours rise above the waterfront in Old Montreal. The original church was built in 1657, but this one replaced it in 1771. Close to the docks, this is where sailors came to pray before and after voyages. Ship models they left as thanks for safe return hang from the chapel's rafters.

Next to the church, on Rue St-Paul, is the Marché Bonsecours, a market building with a silver dome. Made from limestone quarried in Montreal in the 1800s, it was originally a produce market. Today, it is filled with art galleries and small stores selling crafts.

Opposite the Hôtel de Ville is the Château Ramezay, built in 1705 as the home of the eleventh governor of Montreal. When Americans came to Montreal in 1775 to try to convince Montrealers to become American citizens, Benjamin Franklin and Benedict Arnold both stayed there. It is now a museum highlighting eighteenth-century Montreal history.

Notre-Dame-de-Bonsecours (NOH-TRUH-DAHM-DUH-BAWN-SEH-COOR)
Rue St-Paul (REW SAHN-POLE)
Marché Bonsecours (MAR-SHAY BAWN-SEH-COOR)
Château Ramezay (CHAH-TOE RAHM-ZAY)
Rue de Notre-Dame (REW DEH NOH-TRUH-DAHM)
Jean Baptiste (ZHAHN BAHP-TEEST)
St. Sulpice (SAINT SULP-ISS)
Place D'Youville (PLAHSS DYU-VEE)

Marché Bonsecours

The huge Notre-Dame Basilica, on Rue de Notre-Dame West, was built in 1824. Its carved wooden interior has gold trim and the altar is brightly painted and lighted. Behind the altar is a new chapel with a tall modern sculpture at the altar. The bell in Notre-Dame's tower weighs 12 tons. Before it was electrified, it took twelve men to ring it. Montrealers call the bell "Jean-Baptiste" (John the Baptist).

Next to Notre-Dame is the oldest building in the city, the stone St. Sulpice Seminary, built in 1684, only 42 years after the founding of the city. The delicate clock on its tower is thought to be the oldest public clock in North America.

The Montreal History Centre is housed in the old fire station on Place D'Youville. Each room in this museum looks at an era in Montreal's past. The McCord Museum of

Canadian History on Rue Sherbrooke has almost a million photographs, artworks, and artifacts such as furniture, clothes, and toys that show how Canada became the country it is today.

A dinosaur skeleton and a real mummy greet visitors to the Redpath Museum on the campus of McGill University. Science workshops allow visitors to see how scientists learn from the collections, and explore everything from ancient Egypt to how the skeleton of a whale came to be buried under Montreal.

Château Ramezay

McCord Museum Boutique label

OLYMPIC PARK

Olympic Stadium

In 1976, Montreal hosted the Summer Olympic Games and built a beautiful new Olympic Village in the east end of the city. After the Olympics, these buildings were put to other uses. The modern pyramid-shaped dormitory that housed athletes became a fashionable apartment building.

All year round, schoolchildren and their families swim in the stadium, in the same huge pool used by Olympians. The stadium has a high slanted tower that supports the roof. It is the world's largest inclined tower, and everyone enjoys a ride to its top in a cable car for a spectacular view over the top of the city.

The *Jardin Botanique* (Botanic Garden) is one of the largest in the world. There are 26 separate outdoor gardens with more than 26,000 species of plants. The Chinese Garden is the largest outside of China, with a pool, pagodas, and pavilions. Beside it, the Japanese Garden has the largest collection of bonsai (miniature trees) outside of Asia.

*An elegant bloom in
the Botanic Garden*

Jardin Botanique (ZHAR-DAN
BOH-TAH-NEEK)
Biodôme (BEE-OH-DOME)

Ten exhibit greenhouses reproduce different ecosystems needed to grow rare plants from all around the world. Each season has its special exhibits.

The Velodrome, where bicycle races were held, is shaped like a racing helmet. It has been transformed into the Biodôme, a mini-world of four different ecosystems. Here, people can explore a jungle, go walking in a northern forest, explore the St. Lawrence River habitat, and watch penguins, all in the same building and all year round.

The Insectarium, close to the Botanic Gardens and the Biodôme, has a huge collection of insects from all over the world. Exhibits show how bugs behave (how a wasp kills a tarantula, for example). In summer, a special butterfly garden is aflutter with live butterflies. At the end of winter—bug-tasting time—visitors can sample a variety of delicacies including deep-fried bumblebees.

One of the ecosystems in the Biodôme

Winter of Devastation

In early January 1998, a terrible ice storm caused severe damage to trees all over the city, but especially to the forests on Mont-Royal. Cold temperatures at ground level and heavy moisture-filled air passing above combined to coat all of the streets and buildings of the city with more than 6 inches (15 centimeters) of solid ice. The weight of the ice was too much for the trees and tens of thousands of them crashed to the ground. Even when summer leaves cover the remaining trees, the forest shows the effect of that storm.

An autumn view of Beaver Lake at the top of Mont-Royal

MONT-ROYAL, BACKDROP FOR A CITY

The best view of Montreal is from the mountain. From there you can look straight out over the rooftops of all the Plateau neighborhoods and see the tops of the flashy new skyscrapers. On a clear day, the view south over the river and the islands goes to the United States border.

Even though it is in the city, Mont-Royal remains a natural area from its lower slopes to the large cross at its top. The first cross was erected in 1643 by Paul de Chomedey and one has stood there ever since.

A road winds up to the top of the mountain through the forests, leading to miles of walking and hiking trails and to swimming and paddleboats in Beaver Lake. In winter, the lake becomes a skating pond and the hiking trails are filled with cross-country skiers.

A spectacular view of Montreal from the top of Mont-Royal

NEXT-DOOR NEIGHBORS

Montreal is not alone on its island and its island is not alone in the river. West of the Lachine Rapids is the town of Lachine. A museum and an interpretation center there tell the story of the fur trade and the old Lachine Canal. In 2002, the canal will be reopened for pleasure boats to bypass the rapids. The canal's old tow-path is a favorite place for in-line skaters and cyclists.

North of Montreal is Laval, a huge island between Rivière des Prairies and Rivière des Mille Isles. Most of the vegetables and flowers sold in Montreal's markets are grown on Laval's rich farmlands. In summer, Laval is covered with acres and acres of flowers in bloom; in winter, its greenhouses seem ready to burst from the bright colors inside.

A blanket of flowers covers the Nature Center in Laval City.

Even farther north is the year-round resort town of Tremblant. Mont-Tremblant is one of the most popular ski areas in North America. The village looks like a small Alpine town in Europe; ski slopes and trails run right into its main square.

Rivière des Mille Isles
(REEVE-YARE DAY MEE YEEL)

Skiing on Mont-Tremblant

Ski masks like this are worn by skiers the world over, including those who ski on Mont-Tremblant.

TWO ISLANDS, ONE PARK

Today, the twin islands of Notre-Dame and Ste-Hélène are a single park, once called Parc des Îles and now called Parc Jean-Drapeau. Connected to the city by the Metro, bridges, and ferries, these islands are Montrealers' favorite places to play.

Roller coasters at La Ronde, an amusement park built for Expo 67

Both Expo 67 and the Floralies Internationales in 1980, a show-place for gardens from all over the world, left the islands with even more attractions. Acres of beautiful formal gardens from the Floralies brighten the island and include a rare collection of flowers from the far north.

A costumed soldier at the Stewart Museum

The French Pavilion from Expo 67 is now Montreal's Casino and the giant geodesic dome built as the U. S. Pavilion is the Biosphere (easy to confuse with the Biodôme). It is a museum of water that explores the ecosystems of the St. Lawrence River.

The Stewart Museum has a model of the entire old quarter of Montreal, showing with lights and voice description how it has changed. Costumed soldiers reenact drills with cannon and rifle fire, bagpipes and drums. The museum is in a real stone fort built to keep the Americans out. Today, they are welcome.

Montreal children all love La Ronde, the lively amusement park on Île Ste-Hélène that features a multitude of rides, including a Ferris wheel and a roller coaster with loops that turn cars (and passengers) upside down.

Whether they go to ride a roller coaster or a paddleboat, or to kayak, ski, skate or watch soldiers parade to a fife and drum, everyone in Montreal spends some time on the islands in their "front yard."

Summer visitors enjoying the sights on Île Ste-Hélène

Parc des Îles (PARK DAY ZEEL)

FAMOUS LANDMARKS

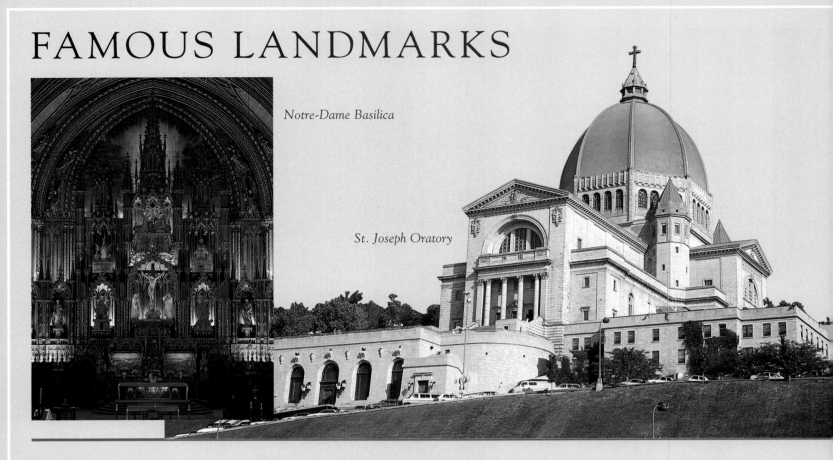

Notre-Dame Basilica

St. Joseph Oratory

Notre-Dame Basilica
A huge gothic-style church built 1824–29, Notre-Dame is well known as the site of a televised Luciano Pavarotti Christmas concert. The massive high altar is painted in many colors and lighted from behind in blue to look like the sky.

Mont-Royal
The 764-foot (233-m) wooded mountain sits right behind the city and forms its backdrop. Trails and a lake for swimming and skating make it a popular place for Montrealers and visitors.

Parc Lafontaine
A major park in a city known for its green space, Lafontaine is close to downtown. With low tree-shaded hills, walking paths, and a meandering pond, it is popular all year round for walking, picnicking, and skating.

Jardin Botanique
One of the largest botanic gardens in the world, Jardin Botanique is also a research institute to preserve rare plant species.

Parc Jean-Drapeau
This park on the islands of Ste-Hélène and Notre-Dame, in the St. Lawrence River, is filled with sports facilities, the gardens of the Floralies, the Biosphere, the Casino, and La Ronde amusement park. Montreal's winter festival is held here.

Hôtel de Ville and Vieux Palais de Justice
The Hôtel de Ville (City Hall) and Vieux Palais de Justice (Old Palace of Justice, or courts of law) look down on the busy Place Jacques Cartier from their parklike setting.

Vieux Montreal
Old Montreal, the original commercial, residential, and religious center of the city, stretches along the riverfront several blocks deep. Among its fine old buildings are a few from the 1600s.

Pointe-a-Calliere Museum of Archaeology and History
A modern structure, this museum is built over the historic heart of the original settlement. Archaeological excavations are enclosed, and visitors can wander on actual streets and see foundations of original guardhouses and homes.

McGill University campus

A view of the Botanical Garden

Pointe-a-Calliere Museum

Biodôme
Inside the former Olympic cycling arena, the Biodôme creates four ecological zones: tropical rain forest, Laurentide forest, the St. Lawrence River, and polar climates of the Arctic and Antarctic. Each is complete with authentic plants and animals.

St. Joseph Oratory
High up on the back of Mont-Royal, the 300 stairs to this pilgrimage site are often climbed by pilgrims on their knees. Miraculous cures have been reported here. A Way-of-the-Cross path is lined with beautiful sculpture at each stop.

Promenade du Vieux Port
The Promenade is a grassy park with sidewalks and bicycle paths along the waterfront from the Lachine Canal to the Clock Tower. Many activities and events take place at the Parc Bassin Bonsecours at the promenade's east end. Piers along the way house the IMAX theater, a mile-long maze shaped like a ship, tour boats, and a brand-new interactive science center..

Place des Arts
Three buildings around an open plaza in the center of downtown Montreal house a symphony orchestra, ballet and opera companies, and a museum of modern art.

McGill University Campus
This top-rated university sits on a large open campus in the heart of the city, on the slopes of Mont-Royal. Its outstanding architecture, the Redpath Museum, and Redpath Concert Hall are attractions there, as is the very realistic statute of founder James McGill.

Musée des Beaux Arts de Montréal
This museum of fine arts has so many fine works that it can exhibit only 5 percent of its permanent collection at any time. Admission is free, but the frequent major visiting exhibitions are not.

FAST FACTS

POPULATION 1996

City 1,016,376
Metropolitan Area 3,326,510

AREA

City 68 square miles (176 sq km)
Metropolitan Area 1,554 square miles (4,025 sq km)

ALTITUDE 187 feet (57 meters)

LOCATION Montreal is on an island in the St. Lawrence River about 165 miles (266 km) west of Quebec City and north of the American states of New York and Vermont. Situated at the Lachine Rapids, its place on the river makes it a major port on the St. Lawrence Seaway between the Atlantic Ocean and the Great Lakes. It is less than one hour by plane from Boston, New York, and Toronto and less than two from Chicago, Washington, D.C., and Philadelphia.

CLIMATE Montreal is on the northern edge of the north temperate zone. In January, temperatures can run from 18 degrees Fahrenheit (–7.7° Celsius) during the day to lows of 18° to 13° F. (–8° to –25° C) at night. In summer, temperatures average about 70° F. (21° C) but can reach 85° F. (30° C) or more. During the spring and fall, temperatures are in the high 60s and low 70s F. (20° to 22° C) during the day and in the low 50s F. (10° to 12° C) at night.

ECONOMY Montreal is an important banking and finance center for the whole of Quebec Province and Canada. Major banks and insurance companies such as Sun Life are located in the city. The Montreal Stock Market is a major player in the world of investment. There is also a large manufacturing segment of the economy, with the Bombardier Corporation, Pratt and Whitney, Canadair, Northern Telecom companies, and a multimedia center located in the city.

CHRONOLOGY

Pre-1500
Algonquin, Huron, and Iroquois live in the area, with the Iroquois mostly south of the St. Lawrence River.

1535
French explorer Jacques Cartier sails up the St. Lawrence to Hochelaga and climbs Mont-Royal.

1603
Samuel de Champlain, another French explorer, arrives at the site of Montreal.

1642
Paul de Chomedey, Sieur de Maisonneuve, founds a missionary colony that becomes a center of the fur trade and commerce with the Native Americans.

1645
Jeanne Mance founds the first hospital in New France.

1655
In order to populate the colony, King Louis XIV of France organizes the export of French orphan girls (*Filles du Roi*) to Montreal.

1658
Marguerite de Bourgeoys founds the first school for women in New France.

1701
A treaty between the French and the Iroquois ends a century of warfare.

1758–1760
Europe's Seven Years' War leads to war between the French and English in North America and to the end of French colonies in Canada.

1775
Montreal is captured by Americans and held until they withdraw in 1776.

1815
First road is completed between Toronto and Montreal.

1824–1829
Notre-Dame Basilica is built.

1847–1849
Britain gradually allows locally elected legislative bodies to assume control over local affairs.

Children among the flowers
at the Botanical Garden

1867
The British North America Act unites four British colonies as the Dominion of Canada; Pierre Chauveau becomes the first premier of Quebec; John A. Macdonald becomes the first prime minister of Canada.

1885
An intercontinental railway from Vancouver, British Columbia, to Montreal is completed, linking Montreal to vast markets in the west.

1890s
Fortunes from trade and railroads lead the wealthy to build new mansions in the Golden Square Mile.

1931
Brother Marie-Victorin achieves a life's dream by opening the Montreal Botanic Garden.

1959
The St. Lawrence International Seaway is completed, opening the Great Lakes to oceangoing ships and changing Montreal's role as a port.

1963
French separatist extremists bomb a Royal Canadian Mounted Police Barracks in the suburb of Westmont.

1967
Montreal hosts the World Exposition, Expo 67, creating a new subway system and Île de Notre-Dame in the process.

1974
French is made the official language of the province.

1977
The use of French is made mandatory in law, government, and business.

1976
The 21st Olympic Games come to Montreal leaving the city with several new athletic facilities.

1980
The Floralies Internationales garden show transforms Île Notre-Dame and creates a new park.

1980
The first referendum on whether to make the Province of Quebec an dependent country is defeated.

MONTREAL

A B C D E F G H I J K

1 2 3 4 5 6 7

MONT-ROYAL PARK

Musée Redpath

Rue Rachel

Rue Roy
THE PLATEAU

Rue Drolet

Parc Lafontaine

Rue Sherbrooke

Musée des Beaux Arts

McGill University

Musée d´Art Contemporain

Rue Sherbrooke
GOLDEN SQUARE MILE

Rue St-Denis

Rue Ste-Catherine

Molson Centre

McCord Museum

Place des Arts

Rue Ste-Catherine

Canadian Center for Architecture

Christ Church Cathedral

CHINATOWN

Rue de La Gauchetière

Hôtel de Ville

Château Ramezay

Chapel of Notre-Dame-de-Bonsecours

ST. LAWRENCE RIVER

Chateau Champlain Hotel

Sun Yat Sen Park
Palais de Justice
VIEUX MONTREAL

Rue St-Paul

Atwater Market

St. Suplice

Notre-Dame Basilica

Rue University

Place Jacques-Cartier

Marché Bonsecours

Jacques Cartier Bridge

La Ronde

Rue de Notre-Dame

Place D'Youville

Parc Bassin Bonsecours

The Stewart Museum

LACHINE CANAL

Montreal History Centre

Musée Pointe-a-Calliere

IMAX

Promenade du Vieux-Port

Parc Jean-Drapeau (Parc des Îles)

ÎLE STE-HÉLÈNE

Biosphere

Maison St-Gabriel

Floralies Gardens

Casino

ÎLE NOTRE DAME

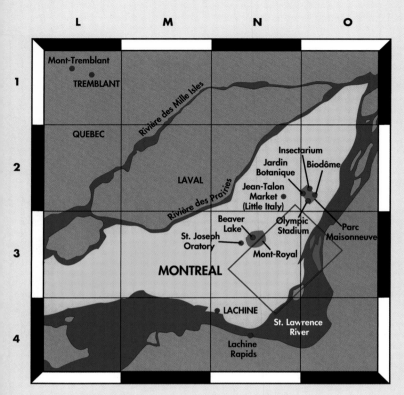

MONTREAL & SURROUNDINGS

GLOSSARY

bonjour: A French word meaning "good day"; used as Americans say "Hello"

coureurs des bois: Literally "runners of the woods," men who went into the forests trapping and trading for fur pelts with the Native Americans

creton: A meat spread, or paté, made of seasoned pork and eaten on French bread

dowry: Money provided by the bride's family at the time of marriage

First Peoples: Canadian term for Native Americans

Francophone: A person whose first language is French

habitants: Middle- and lower-class citizens of the colony of New France, mostly woodsmen, farmers, merchants, and artisans

Hôtel de Ville: City Hall

palisaded: Surrounded by a solid fence of vertical logs

Quebecois: Citizens of the province of Quebec

rue: French for "street"; other streets are sometimes called avenues or boulevards.

Picture Identifications

Cover: Place Jacques-Cartier; the flag of Canada; musician dressed in a traditional French uniform
Page 1: Fleur-de-lis (Quebec symbol) face painting at a Montreal festival
Pages 4-5: A waterfall on Île Ste-Hélène
Pages 8-9: Children among the pumpkins at Atwater Market
Pages 20-21: Samuel de Champlain and his troops during a battle with the Iroquois
Pages 32-33: A face painter painting fleur-de-lis on the cheeks of a young boy during a Quebec Days festival
Pages 44-45: The Chinese Garden in the Botanical Garden

INDEX

Page numbers in boldface type indicate illustrations

To Margie, who loves
Christmas and unicorns, with love –T. K.

For Babs and Becky –A. G.

ALADDIN

An imprint of Simon & Schuster Children's Publishing Division
1230 Avenue of the Americas, New York, New York 10020
First Aladdin hardcover edition September 2020
Text copyright © 2019 by Timothy Knapman
Illustrations copyright © 2019 by Ada Grey
Originally published in Great Britain in 2019 by Egmont UK Limited
For information about special discounts for bulk purchases, please contact
Simon & Schuster Special Sales at 1-866-506-1949 or business@simonandschuster.com.
The Simon & Schuster Speakers Bureau can bring authors to your live event.
For more information or to book an event contact the Simon & Schuster Speakers Bureau
at 1-866-248-3049 or visit our website at www.simonspeakers.com.
Jacket designed by Karin Paprocki
Interior designed by Egmont UK
The text of this book was set in Bembo Infant MT Std and Urbis.
Manufactured in China 0620 SUK
2 4 6 8 10 9 7 5 3 1
Library of Congress Control Number 2020933562
ISBN 978-1-5344-8019-3 (hc)
ISBN 978-1-5344-8020-9 (eBook)

The Twelve UNICORNS of Christmas

Written by
Timothy Knapman

Illustrated by
Ada Grey

ALADDIN

NEW YORK · LONDON · TORONTO

SYDNEY · NEW DELHI

On the **first day** of Christmas,
my parents gave to me . . .

1 sparkling Christmas tree!

On the **fifth day** of Christmas,
my grandma gave to me . . .

5 twinkly unicorn lights!

I hoped Santa would see them
and find his way to our house
on Christmas Eve.

On the **sixth day** of Christmas,
my parents gave to us . . .

6 yummy pies!

My unicorn **loved** the pies. . . .

Uh-oh,
perhaps a bit too much!

On the **seventh day** of Christmas,
my unicorn gave to me . . .

7 wind-up Santas!

So we had a big race.

Ready,

steady,

GO!

On the **eighth day** of Christmas,
my parents made with me . . .

8 snow unicorns!

My snow unicorn was the best . . .

. . . until it fell over!

On the **ninth day** of Christmas, my friends all got from me . . .

9 cards with unicorns on them!

I was being very neat,

but my unicorn loved to scribble
and make a big mess.

On the **tenth day** of Christmas,
my unicorn gave to me . . .

10 cake decorations!

Achoo!

WOW—unicorn sneezes are made of glitter!

On the **eleventh day** of Christmas,
there were some people at the door . . .
11 carol singers!

My unicorn loved singing,
but he wasn't very good at it!

On the night before Christmas,
my unicorn looked a little bit less sparkly . . .

so that night I wished
that Santa would bring
my unicorn a present to
make him feel better.

And when we woke on
Christmas morning,
we heard a funny noise.

So we went downstairs, and you'll **never guess** what we saw. . . .

On the **twelfth day** of Christmas, Santa
brought 11 new friends, so suddenly there were . . .